TABLE OF CONTENTS

WHO ARE MY TEAMMATES?

HUDDLE UP

How would you define the word "revival?"

revival is to come back to health

As Tony Evans said, the issue of racial reconciliation won't be resolved through social structures, but only by God and on his terms. How have you seen that truth being played out in our society lately?

FILM STUDY

STUDY THE PLAYBOOK

Luke 6:12-16

1. What does verse 12 indicate to you about the vitality of Jesus' selection of the right people?
2. What does that verse tell you about the character of Jesus?

JESUS' DEPENDENT RELATIONSHIP WITH THE FATHER

- " … The Son can do nothing by himself; he can do only what he sees his Father doing, because whatever the Father does the Son also does" (John 5:19).
- "For I have come down from heaven not to do my will but to do the will of him who sent me" (John 6:38).
- "No one can come to me unless the Father who sent me draws them … " (John 6:44).

3. Imagine you are one of these chosen disciples. What would you be thinking and feeling? Undeserving? Scared? Honored? Humbled? Loved? Something else?

John 15:9-17

4. Why is love an important key to being part of Jesus' team?
5. In what ways did Jesus choose them and in what ways did they choose to be on Jesus' team?
6. When you choose to be on Jesus' team, what does that imply about who "calls the plays" in your life?
7. How does being under one banner affect how our team works together?

THREE CONVICTIONS OF GREAT TEAMS

DIVERSITY Team: Acts 10:34 and Ephesians 2:14, 19.
Discuss:
- In what ways was Jesus' group diverse?
- Why do you think it took Peter so long to realize what he did in Acts 10?
- How does the Ephesians passage encourage us to treat one another?
- How does diversity make the church stronger and more the way God desires it to be?

LOYALTY Team: John 6:66-69
Discuss:
- What does this passage reveal to you about our choice in being a part of Jesus' team?
- What would it take for the disciples to keep following Jesus even when others were bailing on him?
- In what ways does loyalty build chemistry and cohesiveness on a team?
- How does loyalty make the church stronger and more the way God desires it to be?

MATURITY Team: Acts 5:29, 33, 40-42
Discuss:
- Why would the disciples rejoice after having been flogged?
- How did they demonstrate great maturity as followers of Jesus?
- When life gets tough, how can being part of a group of brave teammates help you to keep standing strong?
- How does maturity make the church stronger and more like God desires it to be?

BREAK THE HUDDLE

MEMORY VERSE
"Every kingdom divided against itself will be ruined; and every city or household divided against itself will not stand."
Matthew12:25

This week, look for ways to build bridges, and unite with others who may look different, act different and be different than you.

NEXT
UP

Complete the six sections in the *Personal Journal* before the next group experience. Use these in your daily time with God over the next six days to help you reflect, evaluate, dig deeper into God's Word and put into practice what you're learning.

WEEK ONE, DAY ONE

Read Psalm 80.

THEME VERSE

"Restore us, O God; make your face shine on us, that we may be saved" (Psalm 80:3).

Welcome to Day 1 of your personal time with God. Through this journal, you will reflect and evaluate, dig deeper into God's Word on specific topics related to spiritual revival and put into practice what you are learning. To begin, write down what you are currently thinking or how are you feeling about the idea of spiritual revival.

The Bible records what some call the greatest breaking-up-and-getting-back-together story ever told. God loves and provides for his people, they eventually take him for granted and wander from him, God does something to get their attention and they come back—or so it appears. Then the cycle starts all over again. 1 Samuel 7:2 is just one place that records an occurrence of reconciliation, restoration and revival: "Then all the people of Israel turned back to the Lord." Where do you think we are in that cycle today? Why?

_____

_____

_____

_____

_____

_____

Today's verse is actually a refrain, repeated three times in Psalm 80 (also in verses 7 and 19). It's the psalmist Asaph's petition to God on behalf of the people of Israel. Restoration means bringing something back to its former, normal or right condition. What do you believe most needs to be restored in the church, nation or world today?

_____

_____

_____

_____

_____

In verse 18, the psalmist says to God, "Revive us, and we will call on your name." _Revive_ means to bring back to life or consciousness. With this in mind, consider the nation, the church, your group, your family, or, most importantly, yourself. What "revival" needs to take place today?

Throughout Scripture, we find God's people praying for revival. This is where it starts! God desires for us to return to him, and he is actively drawing people to himself (John 6:44; 12:32). Look at the following phrases from Psalm 80, and then use them as prompts to write out your own prayer.

- "Hear us, Shepherd of Israel . . . Awaken your might; come and save us" (vv. 1-2).
- "Return to us, God Almighty! Look down from heaven and see! Watch over this vine" (v. 14).
- "Restore us, Lord God Almighty; make your face shine on us, that we may be saved" (v. 19).

WEEK ONE, DAY TWO

Read Acts 19:1-22.

THEME VERSE
"In this way the word of the LORD spread widely and grew in power" (Acts 19:20).

The Book of Acts is a book of revival. A handful of uneducated, ordinary folks who had followed Jesus started a church that turned the world upside-down. Look at just a few of the updates along the way:

- "Those who accepted his message were baptized, and about three thousand were added to their number that day" (Acts 2:41).
- "But many who heard the message believed; so the number of men who believed grew to about five thousand" (Acts 4:4).
- "Nevertheless, more and more men and women believed in the LORD and were added to their number" (Acts 5:14).
- "So the word of God spread. The number of disciples in Jerusalem increased rapidly, and a large number of priests became obedient to the faith" (Acts 6:7).

Imagine what it would be like to be part of a revival like that. How would you feel being involved in a similar spiritual revival today? What part would you play in it?

Part of the revival that took place in Ephesus in Acts 19 occurred as believers were convicted of their wrongdoing, confessed their sins and then turned away from their worldly, evil practices (vv. 18-19). What part must believers play if revival is to happen today?

The revival that took place in Ephesus was described like this: "the word of the Lord spread widely and grew in power." The "word of the Lord" refers to the gospel message that was being preached across the land (see also Acts 6:7; 12:24 and 13:49). What keeps the gospel message from spreading widely and growing in power today? What needs to happen to change the current condition?

Perhaps the revival that occurred in Ephesus can be traced back to the way the apostle Paul prayed for the believers there. Read his prayer, and then use it as a prompt to write your own prayer for your church and/or small group.

"I pray that out of his glorious riches he may strengthen you with power through his Spirit in your inner being, so that Christ may dwell in your hearts through faith. And I pray that you, being rooted and established in love, may have power, together with all the Lord's holy people, to grasp how wide and long and high and deep is the love of Christ, and to know this love that surpasses knowledge—that you may be filled to the measure of all the fullness of God. Now to him who is able to do immeasurably more than all we ask or imagine, according to his power that is at work within us, to him be glory in the church and in Christ Jesus throughout all generations, for ever and ever! Amen" (Ephesians 3:16-21).

WEEK ONE, DAY THREE

Read 1 Corinthians 15:30-34; Proverbs 22:24-25.

THEME VERSE

Do not be misled: "Bad company corrupts good character"
(1 Corinthians 15:33).

For revival to take place, it's vital that you make certain you choose
the right team—Christ's team. It's paramount who you choose to
have on your team as you seek to walk with Christ and carry out
his mission. A modern proverb says, "Your companions are like the
buttons on an elevator. They will either take you up or they will take
you down."

Take some time to evaluate your current traveling companions. Think
of your closest allies. Who takes you up or who takes you down?

What have you seen happen when a Christian surrounds himself or herself with people who do not live Christlike lives? How do they deal with temptation? How well do they grow in becoming more like Christ? How strong and successful is their witness for Christ? How bold are they in proclaiming the Good News?

Do you believe the opposite of today's verse is true? In other words, does good company promote good character? If not, why not? If so, how?

In what *specific* ways do your Christ-following friends (including the people in your group or class) …

- Encourage you (Hebrews 3:13)?

_____

_____

_____

- Spur you on toward love and good deeds (Hebrews 10:24)?

_____

_____

_____

- Pray with and for you that God will open a door for your message and that you will proclaim the Good News clearly to people in your circles of influence? Pray that you will be wise in the way you interact with non-Christians and that you wisely use every opportunity that God gives you (Colossians 4:2-5)?

_____

_____

_____

_____

_____

Now turn the questions above around. Take a moment to reflect on yourself. Are you "good company" for your Christian friends? How would your friends, family members and fellow group members respond to the previous question if they were thinking of you?

_____

_____

_____

_____

_____

Close today's personal time by asking God to help you be the kind of friend others need to help them be strong and courageous followers of Christ and witnesses for him. Open your Bible to Colossians 4:2-6 and use it to prompt you to pray for your friends.

_____

_____

_____

_____

_____

_____

_____

_____

_____

WEEK ONE, DAY FOUR

Read Daniel 3.

THEME VERSE

"Then Nebuchadnezzar said, 'Praise be to the God of Shadrach, Meshach and Abednego, who has sent his angel and rescued his servants! They trusted in him and defied the king's command and were willing to give up their lives rather than serve or worship any god except their own God'" (Daniel 3:28).

Have you counted the cost of being a committed follower of Jesus? For radical disciples of Christ, the possibility or presence of persecution is real (see 2 Timothy 3:12). In fact, Peter called this kind of suffering for being a Christian a "fiery ordeal" (1 Peter 4:12). Shadrach, Meshach and Abednego were three people who counted the cost and found themselves walking literally through a fiery ordeal. Together, these three courageous men stood up to opposition and persecution, and they did not back down (see vv. 16-18).

If you were to go through a "fiery ordeal" because you follow Jesus, what two other people would you want by your side walking through it with you?

Why did you choose them? What is it about their faith, character or commitment that causes you to select them?

Shadrach, Meshach and Abednego went through this fiery ordeal because they refused to worship the idol of their day and resolutely worshiped God alone. What idols in today's world vie for our allegiance to God? And in what ways do people in the world today face persecution if they choose to worship God only?

Billy Graham said, "Courage is contagious. When a brave man takes a stand, the spines of others are often stiffened." It's true. It's always easier to do things when we do them with a friend— whether it's standing up to inequality at work, injustice in the community, insensitivity within your friendship circle, dieting or exercising. Good friends find strength in standing together. How have you seen this principle play out in your life?

In Daniel 3:25, the king saw a fourth man walking in the fire: "Look! I see four men walking around in the fire, unbound and unharmed, and the fourth looks like a son of the gods" (Daniel 3:25). Here in the Old Testament, hundreds of years before Christ came to earth as a man, we have the appearance of God's son. In Matthew 18:20, Jesus promised, "For where two or three gather in my name, there am I with them." God has promised that he will walk through the fiery ordeals and the valleys with us (Psalm 23:4). Sit with that realization for a minute. When you go through difficulties, painful circumstances and persecution, you are not alone. You have friends, including Jesus, with you.

As you close in prayer, keep that realization with you. You are not alone. When you are carrying out his mission, Jesus has promised to be with you always—to the very end. Simply thank him for his presence with you now. Think of a trouble, difficulty or persecution you are going through. What is it?

Thank Jesus that he will go through this with you. Then, if you don't already have them, ask the Lord for two or three faithful friends who will walk with you, as well. Then pray for your friends who may also be going through some fiery ordeals. Ask God to draw close to them and show them that he is beside them.

Today, call a couple friends and let them know you are there for them, no matter how hot it gets!

WEEK ONE, DAY FIVE

Read Acts 2:42-47; 4:32-35.

THEME VERSE
"All the believers were one in heart and mind. No one claimed that any of their possessions was their own, but they shared everything they had" (Acts 4:32).

Unity was a big deal to the early church—so much so that one of Jesus' last prayers was for his followers to be "one" (John 17:20-23). Later, the apostle Paul appealed to the churches to be in unity (e.g., Ephesians 4:11-13). What does "unity" in the church, a Christian group or team look like to you?

The early church shared everything they had with one another (Acts 2:44-45; 4:32, 34, 35). How would that practice bring …

Unity?

Strengthening of community?

Strengthening of the church's witness?

On a scale of zero to four, with zero being "not at all" and four being "totally true," how much do the people in your church share everything they have? (One good test: Are there any needy people among you?)

| 0 | 1 | 2 | 3 | 4 |

Now evaluate your small group or class using the same question:

| 0 | 1 | 2 | 3 | 4 |

What would first need to change to restore the New Testament practice of sharing everything we have?

_____

_____

_____

_____

_____

As you watch most sports, you'll notice athletes wear jerseys that have the team's name on the front and their own last name on the back. A wise coach will remind the players, "We play for the name on the front of our jersey, not the name on the back." In the heat of competition, you make decisions on behalf of the team rather than yourself, as there is a greater cause. The church is a team, filled with all sorts of names and labels, but ultimately the only name that matters is the one on the front of the jersey—and that's the name of Jesus.

How will a focus on Jesus rather than on us create the conditions and opportunity for revival?

Pray today for true unity in your family; your group, class, or team; your church, your city and the country. Pray that God will bring a sense of humility, the desire to put others' needs above your own, a commitment to service and love for one another. As you pray, remember there is absolutely no room for prejudice in an environment of unity. Ask God to rid your church, city and the country of prejudice of all kinds. Ask him to bring you and others together, as only he can, and help all of you share everything with one another, so there are no needy persons among you.

Make this your prayer over the next 24 hours: "May we be one, Father, just as you and Jesus are one!"

WEEK ONE, DAY SIX

Read Acts 1:1-14.

THEME VERSE
You will receive power when the Holy Spirit comes on you; and you will be my witnesses in Jerusalem, and in all Judea and Samaria, and to the ends of the earth" (Acts 1:8).

A common goal can unite a diverse group. We in the church are a diverse group, but we're united by our common goal—to be Jesus' witnesses and make disciples of all nations as we go through our daily lives. Have you ever been a part of a diverse group or team in sports, in school, at work or somewhere else? Think about that experience. What was it like? Did you have a unifying common goal? What were the results?

Jesus gave his followers a compelling, challenging vision of what they would become: his witnesses going near and far with the Good News. Groups, teams, churches and movements need vision. Without it, says Proverbs 29:18, the people are "unrestrained" (NASB) or "run wild" (NLT). Eventually they "perish" (KJV).

Do you know your church's vision statement? Write it below. (If you don't know it, see if you can find it on the church website or ask a church leader.)

Does your group or class have a vision statement? If so, write it down:

Do you have a personal vision for your future? Write it below:

The vision Jesus thrust upon these unschooled ordinary men in Acts 1:8 was an incredible responsibility! The word witness implies far more than just standing up and giving a record of what you have seen and heard. The Greek word is martys, from which we get the

English word "martyr" and the French get their word "marquee." These men were being called to stand out, to be marquees—giant billboards easily seen—and openly announce their dedication to Jesus. They were also called to be martyrs. Every one of these men, with the exception of John, was executed as a result or his companionship with Jesus.

With this in mind, how do you feel about being a witness—a large marquee openly announcing your allegiance to Jesus, or a martyr, prepared to give your life if necessary for your commitment to Jesus and his call?

_____

_____

_____

_____

_____

_____

_____

_____

The diverse group of disciples to whom Jesus first gave this vision and mission would reach people of all nations, races, genders, religious backgrounds, political affiliations and every other diversity (cf. 1 Corinthians 9:19-23). They would, by necessity and as modeled by their Master, reach out to people who were not like them, with whom they didn't agree, whom they were taught as children to despise, who also had prejudices toward them. The vision guided them to look past all these things to see what was ultimately most important: the people's need for Christ.

What will it take for you, your group and your church to look past prejudices to see what is ultimately most important?

_____

_____

_____

_____

_____

What will you do to carry out the vision Jesus gave you? Remember: "It only takes one person to start a revolution."

_____

_____

_____

_____

_____

_____

_____

Acts 1:14 says that these early disciples, to whom Jesus entrusted his vision and mission, "met together and were constantly united in prayer" (NLT). Prayer is the power source for revival. It's vital for you to personally pray for revival and for your group and church to meet together and be united in prayer. Pray today that you and other Christians in your city and around the world will engage in God's vision for revival. Pray first for revival in what is closest to you: yourself, your family, your small group and so forth. Ask God for the humility needed to hear and obey him. Pray also for your leaders, that God will envision, encourage and empower them for his mission.

WHAT WILL IT COST?

HUDDLE UP

What year did you begin to drive? How much did gas cost, if you can remember?

2015

FILM STUDY

STUDY THE PLAYBOOK

Luke 14:25-35

1. How did Jesus define what it means to be his disciple?
2. How do you react internally when you read the word *hate* in verse 26?
3. What consequences result from not counting the cost before building something or engaging in war?
4. In what ways is lukewarm discipleship like unsalty salt?
5. Think back to when you first became a Christian or heard the gospel. What did other Christians tell you about the cost involved?
   - Do you think you received "full disclosure" about all the costs involved? Why or why not?
   - What are the consequences to our faith and the strength of the church when we do not count the cost of being Jesus' disciples?
   - Brainstorm: What are the costs you would tell someone about before or shortly after they made a decision to be a disciple of Jesus?
6. What does it look like in practical terms for a person to make decisions based on being subservient to Jesus' authority?

BREAK THE HUDDLE

Each of us has a vital decision to make: Will I be a part of the crowd, or will I be a true disciple of Jesus? As Hank said in the video, Christianity, like football, requires sacrifice. If I am a real disciple of Jesus, there will be things I will have to give up and leave behind—anything that takes me away from total commitment. Remember: "One hope. One truth. One way."

Dr. Evans pointed out that when we decide every day to follow Christ, our commitment to him is broken down into "bite-sized chunks." What will you do each day this week in order to live surrendered to him?

MEMORY VERSE
"Those of you who do not give up everything you have cannot be my disciples."
Luke 14:33

Look at the following passages that describe the costs and sacrifices associated with following Christ. Pick the one verse that most speaks to you, and reflect on it prayerfully for a few moments.

"No one can serve two masters. Either you will hate the one and love the other, or you will be devoted to the one and despise the other. You cannot serve both God and money" (Matthew 6:24).

"Therefore, I urge you, brothers and sisters, in view of God's mercy, to offer your bodies as a living sacrifice, holy and pleasing to God—this is your true and proper worship. Do not conform to the pattern of this world, but be transformed by the renewing of your mind" (Romans 12:1-2).

"Whatever were gains to me I now consider loss for the sake of Christ. What is more, I consider everything a loss because of the surpassing worth of knowing Christ Jesus my Lord, for whose sake I have lost all things. I consider them garbage, that I may gain Christ and be found in him" (Philippians 3:7-9).

This week, watch for situations in which you can count the cost or make a personal sacrifice as a disciple of Jesus.

NEXT
UP

Complete the six sections in the *Personal Journal* before the next group experience. Use these in your daily time with God over the next six days to help you reflect, evaluate, dig deeper into God's Word and put into practice what you're learning.

WEEK TWO, DAY ONE

Read Matthew 5:1-16.

THEME VERSE
"Blessed are you when people insult you, persecute you and falsely say all kinds of evil against you because of me. Rejoice and be glad … " (Matthew 5:11-12).

Today's passage is from the beginning of the Sermon on the Mount, in which Jesus described in profound language what real discipleship looks like. He turned everything our world teaches us upside-down. He turned "normal" culture on its head. Jesus' teaching separated the "crowds" from his true disciples.

Look back in your Bible to the last three verses in Matthew 4. What were these crowds after? What motives may they have had for following Jesus?

In what ways would Jesus' words at the beginning of the Sermon on the Mount separate the crowd from those committed to him?

Use the following scales to honestly and prayerfully assess yourself (0 = not at all or never; 4 = totally or always):

I am poor in Spirit; I depend completely on God.

0	1	2	3	4

I mourn (in repentance because of my sin).

0	1	2	3	4

I am meek (humble).

0	1	2	3	4

I hunger and thirst for God and his ways of living life the right way.

0	1	2	3	4

I am merciful to others (whether they deserve mercy or not).

0	1	2	3	4

I am pure in heart.

0	1	2	3	4

I am a peacemaker; I seek to restore relationships.

| 0 | 1 | 2 | 3 | 4 |

I am often persecuted and insulted because of my complete commitment to Christ.

| 0 | 1 | 2 | 3 | 4 |

I live *in* the world to make a difference in it, but I am irresistibly different from the world.

| 0 | 1 | 2 | 3 | 4 |

If you heed Jesus' message, you must choose between the culture's values and God's values. Look at the lists below. Which list best describes what you value?

Personal Success	Spiritual Poverty
Freedom of Choice	Mourning
Wealth	Meekness
Power	Mercy/Grace
Recognition	Righteousness
Beauty	Being Pure-hearted
Comfort	Persecution

As you compare these two lists, what can you do today and tomorrow to choose to live according to God's values? What do you need to give up, walk away from or change? What will be your first step(s)?

Living God's way is impossible without God's power. Close your time today by asking him to provide you with the wisdom, strength and fortitude to live his way, regardless of the cost and sacrifice. Admit to him your shortcomings, and turn toward his ways. Ask him to transform your life into what he wants it to be. Remember: It only takes one person to start a revolution.

WEEK TWO, DAY TWO

Read John 15:18-27.

THEME VERSE

"If the world hates you, keep in mind that it hated me first"
(John 15:18).

Jesus spoke the hard truth in love to his followers. People in the world may hate you, not because you are an unlikeable person or have done something reprehensible—unless they equate believing wholeheartedly in Jesus with doing something reprehensible! People may hate you simply because of your decision to be a disciple of Jesus. If you struggle with self-esteem, this truth may be a struggle for you. But this is one big cost for following Jesus: people may not like you; they may even hate you. Sit with that thought for a moment, and dig into your emotions about it. How do you honestly feel, knowing people may hate you because of your commitment to follow Christ?

"If you belonged to the world, it would love you as its own" (v. 19). In what ways do the love, acceptance and admiration of people drive your decisions and actions?

_____

_____

_____

_____

_____

_____

Read and meditate on the following words of Jesus from John 15. Read them as if Jesus were sitting across from you now, looking you in the eyes and saying each of these things to you:

- "As the Father has loved me, so have I loved you. Now remain in my love" (v. 9).

- "I have told you this so that my joy may be in you and that your joy may be complete" (v. 11).

- "Greater love has no one than this: to lay down one's life for one's friends. You are my friend" (vv. 13-14).

- "I chose you and appointed you so that you might go and bear fruit—fruit that will last" (v. 16).

- "Whatever you ask in my name the Father will give you" (v. 16).

- "You do not belong to the world, but I have chosen you out of the world" (v. 19).

Circle any that you especially need to hear from Jesus as opposed to the messages of the world about your identity. Write it/them on an index card, carry it with you and look at it through the day. Or use your mobile device to take a picture of the verse(s) from your Bible and make it the screen saver on your device or computer.

Write out how Jesus feels about you, regardless of how the world feels about you. (If you need more help with this, do an Internet search for "Bible Verses about Our Identity in Christ." One such list is on BibleStudyTools.com.)

_____

_____

_____

_____

_____

_____

Jesus said, "If the world hates you, keep in mind that it hated me first." Why did the world hate Jesus? Because, as Dave said in the video this week, Jesus forces us to choose sides (John 14:6; Acts 4:12). In what ways does being on Jesus' side and knowing that people hate you because of your association with him help you to count the cost of being his disciple?

_____

_____

_____

_____

As you close your time today, simply read and reflect on the prayer Jesus prayed to the Father for his disciples. Allow his prayer to strengthen and encourage you today:

"I am coming to you now, but I say these things while I am still in the world, so that they may have the full measure of my joy within them. I have given them your word and the world has hated them, for they are not of the world any more than I am of the world. My prayer is not that you take them out of the world but that you protect them from the evil one. They are not of the world, even as I am not of it. Sanctify them by the truth; your word is truth. As you sent me into the world, I have sent them into the world. For them I sanctify myself, that they too may be truly sanctified" (John 17:13-19).

WEEK TWO, DAY THREE

Read 1 John 2:15-17; James 4:4; Romans 8:5-11.

THEME VERSE
"Do not love the world or anything in the world" (1 John 2:15).

God's Word warns us that love for, or friendship with, the world's values cannot coexist with our love for God and living according to his values. Our primary allegiance must be to God, his kingdom and his will (Exodus 20:1-3; Matthew 6:33).

Worldliness. Carnality. Life in the flesh. Idolatry. These churchy terms describe a person's life when he or she loves the world and all that is in the world: possessions, power, position, prestige, pride and popularity, just to name of few. These things are temporary (1 John 2:17).

Godliness. Moral purity. Life in the Spirit. God-centeredness. The person who seeks after these values lives forever (v. 17).

Create two lists to contrast what "love for the world" and "love for the Father" look like practically, on a day-to-day basis. If you are to live according to this value, what would your day look like? What would you do or not do, say or not say, think or not think?

LOVE FOR THE WORLD

LOVE FOR GOD

Look through your lists and be purposeful and intentional about your choices.

- From the list on the left, what will you choose to leave behind today? Place an X next to or through that item. What will this choice cost you?

_____

_____

_____

_____

_____

- How will it benefit/bless your life by leaving this behind?

_____

_____

_____

_____

_____

- From the list on the right, choose at least one thing you will choose to take up today. Circle it.

What will this choice cost you?

_____

_____

_____

_____

- How will it benefit/bless your life by choosing to live this way?

_____

_____

_____

_____

_____

_____

Understand: as you make these choices to live fully for God rather than for the world, you enter into a spiritual battle (Galatians 5:16-17; Ephesians 6:10-12; James 4:7-8). This is another cost! But realize you do not fight alone. You have other group members and Christian friends to support you, pray for you, and spur you on. More importantly, you have God's presence and power! You have the power of the Holy Spirit and an army of God's angels protecting you … if you have chosen the right side.

Ask God for his power as you choose to live all-in for him. Ask him to give you the courage you need to choose wisely, the spiritual armor you need to fight, and the strength you need to keep going, regardless of the costs.

_____

_____

_____

_____

WEEK TWO, DAY FOUR

Read Matthew 10:1-23.

THEME VERSE

"I am sending you out like sheep among wolves. Therefore be as shrewd as snakes and as innocent as doves" (Matthew 10:16).

Jesus sent the 12 apostles with some specific instructions and warnings. He told them what kinds of things could happen to them as they went out to teach and minister to people. Note that Jesus told them to go out into the world, not to stay on their comfy couches with one another! He wanted them to go and make a difference in the world, to be irresistibly different.

Imagine you are one of those followers listening to Jesus that day. What would be going through your mind? What would you want to ask or tell Jesus?

Jesus has given us similar instructions and warnings as we go and make disciples. Think about the specific warnings we should be aware of as we go into the world today. Be as specific as you can. Consider some of the recent news stories you've seen or heard. What warnings would Jesus give today?

_____

_____

_____

_____

_____

_____

_____

Within his instructions and warnings to his disciples, Jesus also told them about the resources available as they went out:

> *When they arrest you, do not worry about what to say or how to say it. At that time you will be given what to say, for it will not be you speaking, but the Spirit of your Father speaking through you (Matthew 10:19-20).*

What resources has God already given you for your ministry in the world?

_____

_____

_____

_____

Note the phrase, "Do not worry" in these verses. Do you have any worries about living all-in for Christ and serving him? If so, what are they?

Jesus spoke often about worry. It's one of the things that can keep us from living all-in for him. As we count the costs of being a committed disciple of Jesus, worry is our way of saying, *I'm not sure if I can count this cost. What if something bad happens to me or my family?* It's another way of saying we don't trust God. When Jesus says, "Do not worry," he's saying in effect, "Trust God with this."

If you are honestly ready to do so, complete the sentence below in your own words.

I am, right now, trusting God with and surrendering my worries about …

_____

_____

_____

_____

_____

_____

Use your response to pray about this.

Lord, I trust you. I surrender my worries to you … I want to live all-in for you. I want you to send me, even if that means being sent as a sheep among wolves. Help me to be irresistibly different in the world as I go.

WEEK TWO, DAY FIVE

Read Matthew 16:24-26.

THEME VERSE

"Whoever wants to save their life will lose it, but whoever loses their life for me will find it" (Matthew 16:25).

As Jesus spoke to his disciples about his impending death (Matthew 16:21), he taught them a valuable lesson about the value of life—real life that cannot be lost. He talked about taking up a cross, an instrument of torture and death, and following him. Jesus' words were, and still are, extreme and extremely countercultural.

Jesus also spoke about denying oneself—this is also countercultural in our world today. We are taught to live for ourselves, to indulge in all the pleasures of life. Think for a moment about the messages about the good life you see in the culture: on TV shows and commercials, in magazines and on the Internet, for instance. What does the world teach about life? Try to be specific!

_____

_____

_____

_____

_____

God is not a killjoy. He created the world for us to enjoy. Yet he wants our primary allegiance to be him, not the things of the world.

How we enjoy and how we choose to deny ourselves are largely matters of our attitudes and hearts. Of course, Scripture provides us guidelines for how we enjoy these things. Use the following table to describe how you enjoy (and use wisely) things of the world and how you should choose to deny yourself.

	HOW TO ENJOY	HOW TO DENY SELF
RELATIONSHIPS		
MONEY AND POSSESSIONS		
FOOD		
ENTERTAINMENT (TV, MOVIES, ETC.)		
RECREATION		
OTHER:		

Read John 11:7-16.

Jesus' friend Lazarus was sick, and after waiting two days, Jesus decided to go to him. But this created a problem for his disciples. It wasn't safe for them to go back to Judea. At least some of the disciples worried about what might happen and made excuses not to go. We are faced again with the choice of worrying or trusting. In verse 16 of this passage, Thomas finally stood up and decided to trust God, no matter what it cost. Jesus said, "Let's go" (v. 15), and Thomas, said, "I'm right behind you, Jesus."

What does it take to have that kind of devotion and courage in the face of danger?

At first some of the other disciples made excuses. Jesus was used to hearing excuses from people:

> A teacher of the law came to him and said, "Teacher, I will follow you wherever you go." Jesus replied, "Foxes have dens and birds have nests, but the Son of Man has no place to lay his head." Another disciple said to him, "Lord, first let me go and bury my father." But Jesus told him, "Follow me, and let the dead bury their own dead" (Matthew 8:19-22).

Have you ever made excuses for not going all-in as a disciple of Jesus? What are some of them?

Consider those excuses that you or others make for not being fully committed to following Jesus. Think about how those are ways of saving your life rather than losing your life for Jesus.

What would it mean today to lose your life for Jesus?

It's one thing to say, "I'll take up my cross and follow you, Jesus; I trust you with my life; I'll follow you, even if that means I die for you." It's another thing to follow through on that commitment when your life is on the line. Thomas, as well as the other disciples, went to Judea with Jesus, but most of them ran and hid when Jesus was arrested. When Jesus was in the garden praying, they all fell asleep!

Prayer is your power source for living according to your commitments. Pray today that God will empower you and encourage you if you ever find yourself in a setting when your life is on the line.

WEEK TWO, DAY SIX

Read Revelation 2:8-11.

THEME VERSE

"Do not be afraid of what you are about to suffer … Be faithful, even to the point of death, and I will give you life as your victor's crown" (Revelation 2:10).

Take a moment and honestly assess how you feel about death. Do you fear it? Do you worry about it? Do you have unanswered questions or doubts?

In response to those fears, worries, questions and doubts, Jesus says:

> *Do not be afraid. Do not worry. Do not back down or give up.*
> *Be faithful.*

Jesus warned the church of ancient Smyrna, and the church of today, about what was going to happen to them because of his Name. They would suffer. He also reminded them about their response as his church—to simply be faithful to the end, no matter what. Then—and don't miss this—he gave them a promise: he will give them, and us, life. Abundant life. Eternal life. A life that can't be taken away from us. And when we've run the race, we'll receive a victor's crown!

Jesus' view of death is countercultural, as well. Back in John 11, Jesus told Lazarus' sister Martha, "I am the resurrection and the life. The one who believes in me will live, even though they die; and whoever lives by believing in me will never die. Do you believe this?" (vv. 25-26).

How would you summarize how Jesus wants us to think about and feel toward life and death?

_____

_____

_____

_____

Perhaps death is the biggest and the seemingly final cost of being a disciple of Jesus. The apostle Paul knew this. He wrote,

"When the perishable has been clothed with the imperishable, and the mortal with immortality, then the saying that is written will come true: "Death has been swallowed up in victory."

"Where, O death, is your victory?
     Where, O death, is your sting?" (1 Corinthians 15:54-55)

Jesus and Paul both talked about victory in death. Imagine your own tombstone for a moment. Etched upon it is one word in bold letters: "VICTORIOUS." What would you want people who know you best to say to others in explanation of that word on your tombstone?

_____

_____

_____

_____

_____

_____

_____

"Be joyful in hope, patient in affliction, faithful in prayer" (Romans 12:12).

Faithfulness to God becomes more natural as you spend time with the Father. Begin by being faithful to him by abiding with him each day in prayer. As you close out this week of your personal time with God, thank him for his faithfulness to you. Ask him to increase your faith and take away any areas of unbelief.

CAN I MAKE A DIFFERENCE?

GROUP TIME

HUDDLE UP

Think of a time in your life when someone recognized a gift or talent you have and encouraged you to make a difference. Who was it and what did they tell you?

FILM STUDY

STUDY THE PLAYBOOK

DISCOVERY

"As Jesus was walking beside the Sea of Galilee, he saw two brothers, Simon called Peter and his brother Andrew. They were casting a net into the lake, for they were fishermen. 'Come, follow me,' Jesus said, 'and I will send you out to fish for people.' At once they left their nets and followed him" (Matthew 4:18-20).

1. As Peter began following Jesus, how do you envision Peter as he continued to discover his gifts and what God eventually would call him to do?

DEVELOPMENT

2. What teachable moments can you think of that Jesus used to develop the twelve apostles, especially Peter?

- Matthew 14:28-33
- Matthew 16:13-19
- Matthew 16:20-23
- Matthew 26:31-35, 69-75
- John 21:15-19

DIVING IN

"Then Peter stood up with the Eleven, raised his voice and addressed the crowd: 'Fellow Jews and all of you who live in Jerusalem, let me explain this to you; listen carefully to what I say'" (Acts 2:14; also see vv. 37 and 41).

3 How had Jesus prepared Peter for just this moment?

Acts 4:1-22

4 What were the results of the healing and Peter's preaching on this occasion?

5 From where did Peter and John get their courage, boldness and power to do the extraordinary?

6 Do you believe spiritual revival can happen today and that God can use you? Which of the following choices best describes your thoughts and feelings today?

- I'm a bit like Coach Gerelds. I'm kind of cynical. I'm not sure if it's all real or not.
- To tell the truth, I've gotten used to playing it safe over here on the bench. I'm comfortable.
- I'm still a bit skeptical, but I could be convinced it could happen today.
- Like Coach Stearns, I'm taking a look around me and at what God is doing. I'm in.
- I'm a crooked stick that God can use to hit his bulls eye. I'm ready to be used to make an impact!
- Other:

BREAK THE HUDDLE

One of the most powerful moments in the video was toward the beginning. It's when Hank the chaplain called out Tony and brought him face to face with his giftedness. Like Tony, God has given each one of us a gift.

It's up to each of us to accept the gift God has given us and to use it for something higher than ourselves. As Tony Evans said, "When you say, 'Lord, how can you use the gifts, talents, skills, and abilities you've endowed me with for your purposes?' you'll be blessed because you'll be fulfilled, he'll be glorified, and people will be benefited."

This week, watch for opportunities in which you can allow God to take your ordinary gifts and do something extraordinary so that when people look at your life they see Jesus.

MEMORY VERSE

"When they saw the courage of Peter and John and realized that they were unschooled, ordinary men, they were astonished and they took note that these men had been with Jesus" (Acts 4:13).

NEXT UP

Complete the six sections in the *Personal Journal* before the next group experience. Use these in your daily time with God over the next six days to help you reflect, evaluate, dig deeper into God's Word and put into practice what you're learning.

WEEK THREE, DAY ONE

Read 1 Peter 4:7-11.

THEME VERSE
"Each of you should use whatever gift you have received to serve others, as faithful stewards of God's grace in its various forms," (1 Peter 4:10).

In the small group session, you studied the life and spiritual development of the apostle Peter. Later in his life, Peter wrote the directions you are studying today. He was simply sharing with his fellow Christ followers what he had learned from his time with Jesus years before.

As we live for Christ with the recognition that he may return at any time, Peter tells us several things we should keep doing:

- Stay alert
- Pray
- Love one another
- Be hospitable to others
- Use the gift God gave you to serve others
- Let God speak through you
- Serve others so God may be praised

How much are each of these a part of your everyday lifestyle? Which of these are you doing well? In which do you need to mature? Honestly evaluate yourself in your own words.

Look again at verse 10. When you view the spiritual gifts God gave you, as well as the personality, abilities and passions God gave you, as a steward—that is, as someone the Master has entrusted to develop, use and multiply them for his glory—how does that motivate you to do something that will make a difference with those gifts?

knowing he gave me the gift of counseling i feel honored. I get to help people feel better emotionally & while talking, its a perfect time to share Gods grace!

What will it look like today for you to use your gifts, abilities, personality and passions to be a steward of God's grace at home, at work or school, in your neighborhood or with specific family members or friends?

use my gift to help those I love to feel better emotionally & come to terms

Reread and focus on the words of this verse:

> "If anyone speaks, they should do so as one who speaks the very words of God. If anyone serves, they should do so with the strength God provides, so that in all things God may be praised through Jesus Christ. To him be the glory and the power for ever and ever. Amen" (1 Peter 4:11).

Peter may have been thinking about the life principles he had learned from Jesus when he said:

> "I do nothing on my own but speak just what the Father has taught me" (John 8:28).

> "By myself I can do nothing; I judge only as I hear, and my judgment is just, for I seek not to please myself but him who sent me" (John 5:30).

Close your time today in worshipful prayer. Use the following prayer starters to lead you:

- Thank you, Lord, for the gifts, abilities, personality, passions and life situations you have uniquely given me …
- May you be praised, God, through my actions and words today …
- May all the glory go to you, Father, as I serve others today …

Read 1 Corinthians 12:12-27.

THEME VERSE

"Now you are the body of Christ, and each one of you is a part of it" (1 Corinthians 12:27).

As you studied in Day One, God has given you a spiritual gift as well as unique abilities, a unique personality, unique passions and unique life situations. Today you see that those are all given to you in a unique environment: the church. You play a part on a team—a necessary part, a vital part. Your group would not be the same without you. In fact—and this is difficult for people to see sometimes, but it's true—God's church would not be the same without you.

What would your small group or class miss if you were not part of it?

They would miss my advice & words of comfort

What would your local church miss if you were not a part of it?

How would God's global church be different if you were not part of it?

Even though you don't always notice it, God is working through all the circumstances and situations of your life to carry out his purposes:

> "But in fact God has placed the parts in the body, every one of them, just as he wanted them to be" (v. 18).

For what reasons might God have placed you in your group, church, workplace, neighborhood or circle of friends?

maybe to help them cope & figure out how to deal w/ their problem

In a parallel passage in Romans 12 the apostle Paul said,

> "In Christ we, though many, form one body, and each member belongs to all the others" (v. 5).

Consider what it means for you to "belong" to your brothers and sisters in Christ and for them to "belong" to you. With that in mind, what will you do for members of your group, class or church this week to encourage them to use their gifts for God's glory?

Lift them up & encourge who they are
Be there for them & hear them out.

Close your time today praying for your fellow group or church members. Ask God to draw them closer to him and help them see their unique places in his body.

WEEK THREE, DAY THREE

Read 1 Samuel 17:1-50.

THEME VERSE
"This day the Lord will deliver you into my hands, and I'll strike you down … and the whole world will know that there is a God in Israel" (1 Samuel 17:46).

The locker room scene, before Woodlawn faced the seemingly unbeatable Huffman team, was another powerful moment in the video. Allyson and Tony each read parts of the familiar story of David and Goliath. Hank continued the story, telling the team they would win the game—because it wasn't about them. They'd win, they'd do the impossible, so all would know about the God they believed in.

Think of an "impossible" situation, the "giant" in your own life. What is it?

_____

_____

_____

The attitude of all the "real" soldiers in Israel's army that day on the battlefield was to look at Goliath and say, "He's so big, we'll never get him." But David saw how big his God was—and that was all that mattered to him. What has your attitude been toward the "giant" in your life? Do you tend to look at how big or impossible it seems? Why?

What resources do you need to take on this giant in your life? Earlier in the story, David tried putting on Saul's armor, but it didn't fit. Not only that, but if he used Saul's armor and weapons, people may have said, "Oh, it was the armor; it was the superior craftsmanship of the weapons David used." So be careful about what weapons you decide to fight with. God will you give you all the weapons you need for your battle (see Ephesians 6:10-18). So think about the resources God has given you: people in your small group or church, for instance; God's Word; prayer.

What do you need to fight your giant?

I would need strength, will, encouragement + maybe help from others

Regardless of the final outcome of this situation—your battle with this giant—how might it bring glory to God? How can it show people around you that there is a loving, life-giving, all-powerful God who you believe in?

If you over come it you can explain that God was the one that gave you youre extra Strength & will

The battle cry for the Woodlawn team was "On this day!" We have a tendency to procrastinate when it comes to battling giants. We might be happy to take a stand for Jesus—but does it have to be today? Yet there comes a time when you have to leave the locker room and enter the battle. The Holy Spirit will never say, "Tomorrow." He will always say "Today." God's Word says, "Indeed, the 'right time' is now. Today is the day of salvation" (2 Corinthians 6:2, NLT).

Close your time in prayer with that sense of urgency. If you still have a decision to make about accepting Jesus Christ as your Savior, give yourself to him on this day. If you are ready to commit yourself to him as the Lord and leader of your life, do it *on this day*. Seek out a Christian friend or leader and talk to them. If you are ready to step up and fight that giant, go in the name of the God of the angel armies and for his glory—on this day!

WEEK THREE, DAY FOUR

Read Mark 9:14-29.

THEME VERSE

" … Anything is possible if a person believes" (Mark 9:23).

"Impossible" is not in God's vocabulary. Throughout the Bible, God does what people think can't be done.

While Jesus was on the mountain with Peter, James and John—as well as Moses and Elijah, by the way—the rest of the apostles were in the town arguing with some religious leaders. They had tried to heal a boy who was demon-possessed, but failed. The boy's dad, obviously frustrated by the events so far, turned to Jesus. " … Have mercy on us and help us, if you can," said the boy's father. (v. 22).

Jesus retort is classic: "What do you mean, 'If I can?'" Jesus asked. "Anything is possible if a person believes" (v. 23).

We may be able to learn something from the dad's response: "I do believe, but help me overcome my unbelief!" (v. 24).

Do you identify with the dad in this story? Do you believe in God, the Father, Son and Holy Spirit? Do you believe Jesus is the Christ, the Son of God and your Savior? Do you believe all these facts about Jesus and yet still struggle with unbelief when it comes to those giants in your life? Take some time right now to identify any areas of unbelief you have.

I do have uncertainities & struggle w/ doubt

Perhaps you've moved out of the realm of "impossible" and now, like the dad, you still "kinda believe." You have an "if you can" kind of faith. If that describes you, do as the dad did, and ask Jesus to help you overcome your unbelief. Write out your request of Jesus:

Dear God, i have my grants and i want to put all my faith in you that you will help me in my fight but i struggle with thoughts of doubt. i want to be confident & give full faith. Please help me overcome my unbelief & let me dive whole heartedly into you.

Even biblical heroes sometimes doubted if God could or would come through.

> When Abraham and Sarah doubted if God could really bring them their promised son, God said, "Is anything too hard for the Lord?" (Genesis 18:14).

When Moses questioned whether God could really provide enough meat for his entire army of 600,000 men, God asked him, "Is the LORD'S arm too short?" (Numbers 11:23).

When Jesus' disciples wondered if a rich person could be saved, Jesus stated, "With man this is impossible, but with God all things are possible" (Matthew 19:26).

How do you think God would respond to you right now as you deal with a difficult, trying, painful situation in your life? Would he ask:

- Is anything too hard for me?
- Is my arm too short?
- With people, this is impossible, but with me, all things are possible.
- Other:

Each of the Bible heroes eventually trusted God to do what only he could do. What do you need to trust God with right now? Jot that down and then write out your prayer of trust.

I need to trust God with his plan for me & that he will guide me in the correct path & that I will soon find my true purpose

The apostle Paul said he had learned the secret of being content in any life circumstance. Many people would spend a lot of money for just one moment of pure contentment! What was Paul's secret? He said, "I can do all things through him who gives me strength." It was the power of Christ inside of him that gave him all the contentment he needed. Do you need Christ's strength as you deal with a difficult circumstance in your life? Do you need his power as you face that giant?

Close in prayer, recognizing Christ's presence and power with you right now, where you are. Praise him for being the all-powerful, all-knowing God that he is. A humble yet powerful prayer is to simply tell him that with your own ordinary human strength this is impossible, but with God all things are possible. *Nothing* is impossible with God!

WEEK THREE, DAY FIVE

THEME VERSE

"And who knows but that you have come to your royal position for such a time as this?" (Esther 4:14)

In the video for this week, Dave quickly mentioned three Old Testament heroes who were at first reluctant to live out God's purpose for their lives. Yet each one eventually stepped up—even with sweaty palms and shaky legs—and was used by God in a significant way to make a difference in the world. Read each of the following three sets of passages and see who and what you identify with. (If you have time, also read the surrounding and omitted verses for context.)

MOSES
Read Exodus 3:9-14; 4:1, 10-13.
God had appeared to Moses in a bush that was on fire but didn't
burn up (v. 2) and then told Moses exactly who he was (vv. 5-6).
Yet Moses balked when God told him how he would use Moses to
make a difference. Moses tried several excuses to get out of what
God was clearly calling him to do. Have you ever made similar
excuses? In what ways can you relate to these?

- Who am I that I should go and do this? (I don't have the
  right personality, education, background, ministry experience …)

- What would I even say if they asked me questions? (I don't
  know enough about the Bible or doctrine yet.)

- What if … ? (I'm afraid what will happen if I take on this
  assignment. I feel like I wouldn't be in control.)

- I've never been good at talking to people. (I have a legiti-
  mate disability that keeps me from serving you.)

- Please send someone else. (You've got the wrong person.)

What do God's responses tell you about the legitimacy of these
excuses?

GIDEON
Read Judges 6:12-16, 22-24, 36-40; 7:17-25.

Gideon was a man of reason. When the angel of the Lord told him what he was being called to do, Gideon at first had a number of logical rationales for why the Lord's plan wouldn't work. Notice that in both Moses' and Gideon's cases, their excuses dealt with what they could or couldn't do, but the Lord response was what *he* would do.

Gideon's first argument had to do with what he perceived God had done or hadn't done in the past. "Why has all this happened to us?" he asked. How have you seen these kind of "why" questions affect the responses of people, including yourself, to do something about the needs in the world?

_____

_____

_____

_____

_____

_____

_____

God reduced Gideon's army from 32,000 to 300 (7:1-7). God told Gideon that he had too many men for God to carry out his plan. Sometimes we rely on our own limited resources too much for God's unlimited power to work and for his glory to be seen. God's power is made perfect in our weakness (2 Corinthians 12:9-10). What human strengths or resources are you depending on more than God's power? What do you need to let go of so God can work through you?

_____

_____

_____

_____

_____

_____

Look at the encouraging words of the angel of the Lord to Gideon in Judges 6:

"The Lord is with you, mighty warrior" (v. 12).

"Go in the strength you have ... Am I not sending you?" (v. 14).

"I will be with you" (v. 16).

" ... Peace! Do not be afraid. You are not going to die" (v. 23).

What encouragement do you need to hear from God or others to step up in God's power to make a difference?

_____

_____

_____

_____

_____

ESTHER
Read Esther 4.
What were Esther's fears?

_____

_____

_____

_____

Esther was able to move forward and accept her responsibility to make a difference by realizing she had been put in her life circumstance "for such a time as this" and through fasting prayer.

Close your time today in prayer. If you, like Esther, are dealing with any fears in stepping up to make a difference, consider fasting about this so you can focus on God during this time. Prayerfully consider the place in life where God has placed you—in your family, workplace, neighborhood, small group or circle of friends, for instance. What are the needs around you? In what ways can God use you to make a difference at such a time as this? Ask God for his strength to respond.

_____

_____

_____

_____

_____

_____

WEEK THREE, DAY SIX

Read Philippians 2:12-18.

THEME VERSE

"It is God who works in you to will and to act in order to fulfill his good purpose," (Philippians 2:13).

God is working in you, through his Spirit, helping you "want to do and be able to do what pleases him" (v. 13, New Century Version). God gives you both the desire and the ability to carry out his purposes through your life. That makes it pretty difficult to make excuses or to reason away his call to make a difference! Not only that, God promises to be with you as you go, to protect you and to empower you. But like a TV pitchman, the Bible says, "But wait! There's more!"

> "For we are God's handiwork, created in Christ Jesus to do good works, which God prepared in advance for us to do," (Ephesians 2:10).

Look at the following word study for this verse:

- Handiwork = "workmanship" (KJV), "masterpiece" (NLT), "creation" (HCSB). God has made us what we are. The Greek word is *poiema*, from which we get our English word, "poem."

- Created = brought into being or originally founded. It takes on the sense of proprietorship or ownership of the manufacturer.

- Which God prepared in advance for us to do = literally, "which God did before prepare, that in them we may walk" (*Young's Literal Translation*). The idea is that these good works become our lifestyle, not just something we do every once in a while. A good translation is "which God planned in advance for us to live our lives doing" (NCV).

How does this information add to how you understand and apply this verse?

You are God's handiwork, his masterpiece, his poem to the world. Sit with that reality for a few moments. Let it sink into your brain and your soul.

If you struggle with how you view yourself, write these words on your mirror or on a card and put it where you can see it every day:

I am God's handiwork.
I am God's masterpiece.
I am God's poem to the world.

Write below how you will choose to accept those words.

When God created you, he did so with a reason, for a purpose. But accepting that purpose is up to you! By the way, don't worry about knowing what that purpose is or for God's specific will for your life. He'll make it known to you as you spend time with him in personal Bible study, in prayer, as you spend time with other Christ followers and especially as you serve. Look around you. What needs do you see in the environment where God has placed you?

As you close in prayer, determine today to allow God to work in you to will and to act to fulfill his good purpose. No more excuses or reasons for not making a difference. On this very day say "yes" to God. Yes, Lord. Send me!

"Through Jesus, therefore, let us continually offer to God a sacrifice of praise—the fruit of lips that openly profess his name. And do not forget to do good and to share with others, for with such sacrifices God is pleased," (Hebrews 13:15-16).

WHERE IS MY IDENTITY?

HUDDLE UP

When you hear the word *surrender*, what do you usually think of?

FILM STUDY

STUDY THE PLAYBOOK

2 Corinthians 5:14-21

A NEW PERSPECTIVE

A NEW PATHWAY

NEW PURPOSES

1. What's the difference between being rehabilitated and being re-created?

2. What's the difference between living your life *for* Christ or *with* Christ and living your life *in* Christ?

3. What would it look like if each one of us applied this passage in our lives this week?

BREAK THE HUDDLE

How can you be an ambassador, that is, a representative of King Jesus, this week?

What would it look like for God to make his appeal for reconciliation through you this week?

To whom would God make his appeal?

MEMORY VERSE
"Therefore, if anyone is in Christ, the new creation has come: The old has gone, the new is here!" (2 Corinthians 5:17)

NEXT UP

Complete the six sections in the Personal Journal before the next group experience. Use these in your daily time with God over the next six days to help you reflect, evaluate, dig deeper into God's Word and put into practice what you're learning.

WEEK FOUR, DAY ONE

Read Ephesians 2:1-5.

THEME VERSE
"The god of this age has blinded the minds of unbelievers, so that they cannot see the light of the gospel that displays the glory of Christ, who is the image of God" (2 Corinthians 4:4).

As you seek to live in Christ as a new creation in him—as you trust him to live day by day with a new perspective on a new pathway with new purposes—it's vital for you to recognize that you have an enemy who will throw everything he can at you to try to get you to go back to your old ways. Jesus identified him as a thief who has come only to steal, kill and destroy (John 10:10) this new life you're living. Your new life is a threat to him and his kingdom.

How does Paul identify people before they give their lives to Christ?

Who do they follow, even if not purposely? What do these verses tell you about the nature of the world in which we live?

Paul was writing primarily to Christians. Note the verb tenses: *were, used to live, followed,* etc. Also note the change in verb tenses in verse 4. What main message was Paul sending to these people in the church?

One of Satan's approaches is presented in today's theme verse: 2 Corinthians 4:4. What are some ways that Satan blinds people to God's light, love and glory today?

Because of Jesus' substitutionary death for us, when God looks at you, he sees his son, Jesus. He sees you as his child (see Galatians 4:4-7). But that's not how Satan wants you to see yourself. As Dave said, Satan sees you by your sin and that's how he wants you to see yourself. His "identity theft" is not new.

He tried it with Job in the Old Testament. Here's how God saw Job:

" ... There is no one on earth like him; he is blameless and upright, a man who fears God and shuns evil" (Job 1:8).

Satan proposed to God a test of Job's identity:

"But now stretch out your hand and strike everything he has, and he will surely curse you to your face" (v. 11).

Satan took nearly everything away from Job, leaving him sitting in a pile of dust and ashes, suffering physically and emotionally. Satan wanted to steal Job's identity as "blameless" and "upright" and replace it with "God curser." He was unsuccessful.

It's difficult, if not impossible, for us to understand what is going on in the spiritual realms as we deal with adversity, loss and pain. How does Job's story help you continue to trust God when life circumstances are difficult?

_____

_____

_____

_____

_____

In the New Testament, Satan tried to steal even Jesus' identity as God's Son, Messiah and Redeemer (Matthew 4:1-11). Satan's tactic was to try to get Jesus to focus on himself, his physical needs and the world.

Jesus depended on the Holy Spirit and Scripture. How can you utilize these two God-given resources as you battle Satan's plans to steal your identity?

_____

_____

_____

The good news is that you are not unaware of Satan's schemes (2 Corinthians 2:11). You also know how to resist him:

"Submit yourselves, then, to God. Resist the devil, and he will flee from you. Come near to God and he will come near to you" (James 4:7-8).

Close in prayer, taking this opportunity to "come near to God." As you pray, reflect on how God sees you as his loved, cherished, gifted child. Ask him to help you see yourself as he sees you.

WEEK FOUR, DAY TWO

Read Romans 8:1-2, 31-39.

THEME VERSE

" … There is now no condemnation for those who are in Christ Jesus … " (Romans 8:1).

As you saw on Day One, Satan wants you to return to your old self, to wear a nametag that says "Sinner" or "Deserving of Wrath" or "Condemned." But that's what you *were*, not who you *are*, if you are in Christ Jesus. Remember: "The old has gone, the new is here!" (2 Corinthians 5:17). When you come to Christ, it doesn't mean you'll be sinless, but the closer you draw to Christ, you should sin less and less and less.

So, amid all the accusations from Satan and the world, the Creator says to you clearly, "There is now no condemnation for those who are in Christ Jesus."

The question is this:
Who are you going to listen to?

Take a moment and just dwell on that question. Is your response easy or difficult? Why? What will it take to listen to the truth?

_____

_____

_____

_____

_____

_____

_____

Read Romans 8:31-39 again. Read it several times if you need to. Circle or underline in your Bible any phrases that stand out to you. Write them below and then describe *why* those phrases mean something to you. What need in you do they fill? What do they say that you need to hear?

_____

_____

_____

_____

_____

_____

One of the identities that God wants you to adopt is the name LOVED. He says in this passage, and throughout the Bible, "You are loved." In fact, there is absolutely nothing in the world—including demons—that can take that name away from you.

Write a short note accepting God's love for you and the identity he has given you. Thank him for it.

Because God loves you and is for you, you are a conqueror over anything Satan or the world tries to throw at you. The Bible tells us that even though we may go through difficult times in this life, and even though Satan may seem to be gaining traction in the world, we who are in Christ Jesus will be victorious! This is another part of your identity; you are a SUPER CONQUEROR! You are a VICTOR.

As you accept your identity in Christ, how else do you want to respond to God? Write it out as a prayer.

WEEK FOUR, DAY THREE

Read Jeremiah 29:10-14.

THEME VERSE

"You will seek me and find me when you seek me with all your heart," (Jeremiah 29:13).

Do you identify at all with Coach Gerelds or Johnnie in the movie? Are you seeking God? Maybe you have not yet accepted Jesus as your Savior; you still have some unanswered questions or something else that's holding you back. That's OK; keep seeking, but don't procrastinate! Or maybe you have accepted Jesus as Savior, but you realize with increasing clarity that there's more than that. You're seeking a deeper, richer relationship with him and maybe you need to make him the Lord of your life.

The truth is, even if you are a mature Christian, you're still seeking a deeper, more abiding relationship with God each day. No matter who you are and where you are, today's Bible passage is full of promises to embrace, as well as some vital responsibilities on your part.

The specific promise in verse 10 of this passage refers to the seventy years of judgment that God had placed on Judah (cf. Jeremiah 25:11-12; 2 Chronicles 36:21; Daniel 9:2). But we can certainly apply these promises to our own lives today.

What does it look like for you to seek God "with all your heart?"

When you seek him with all your heart, God promises that he will be found by you. He wasn't hiding in the first place. In fact, he has been seeking you, drawing you to him:

"I have loved you with an everlasting love; I have drawn you with unfailing kindness" (Jeremiah 31:3).

"No one can come to me unless the Father who sent me draws them ... " (John 6:44).

"And I, when I am lifted up from the earth, will draw all people to myself" (John 12:32).

So, God is not the one playing hide and seek—we are! Humans have been trying (unsuccessfully) to hide from God since Adam and Eve in Genesis 3. We hide because we're ashamed of ourselves, but God says, "I've loved you with an everlasting love; I've drawn you with unfailing kindness!"

How have you sensed God drawing you to him lately? Who or what is he using?

Regardless of where you are on your search, God already has plans for you and your future. He has given you the gift of free will to either disregard him and his plans for you or to willingly accept them. What hope does Jeremiah 29:11 give you as you seek God?

One of the best promises in the Bible has to do with the fact that God desires to have a relationship with you. He says,

> "Then you will call on me and come and pray to me, and I will listen to you" (v. 12).

As you call on God today, as you come to him and pray to him, he is listening to you. Knowing he is present with you and is listening attentively to you, what do you want to say to him?

WEEK FOUR, DAY FOUR

Read Romans 5.

THEME VERSE

"Therefore, since we have been justified through faith, we have peace with God through our Lord Jesus Christ" (Romans 5:1).

Justification. It may be a big, churchy sounding word, but it also represents a fundamental doctrine for Christ followers to understand. Romans 5 may seem at first like a deep, theological passage that's difficult to comprehend, but it provides some of the most foundational teachings in the Bible about your faith and your identity.

Dave talked about justification in the video this week. He said the word itself helps us understand its meaning. It means "just as if I never sinned." The *Merriam-Webster Dictionary* defines *justify* as "to prove or show to be just, right or reasonable." The Greek word was a legal term that meant to render just or innocent, to declare someone righteous and to regard as innocent. Note an important distinction in how the word is used. It means to *declare* or *regard* someone as innocent, not to *make* them innocent. God declares us innocent, even though, in reality, we are guilty of our sins.

God treats you *just as if* you've never sinned. As far as the east is from the west, so far has he removes our transgressions from us (Psalm 103:12). How does this truth resonate with you? Do you easily accept this good news as the truth, or do you struggle with it? Why?

_____
_____
_____
_____
_____
_____

Read the following verses from Romans about justification. As you do, circle the words *through* and *by*.

"Therefore, since we have been justified through faith, we have peace with God through our Lord Jesus Christ" (5:1).

"Since we have now been justified by his blood, how much more shall we be saved from God's wrath through him!" (5:9)

"For all have sinned and fall short of the glory of God, and all are justified freely by his grace through the redemption that came by Christ Jesus" (3:23-24).

What does this teach you about *how* (through or by what) we receive justification?

_____
_____
_____
_____
_____
_____

The effects of this justification on our lives are incredible:

- Peace with God (v. 5:1)
- Saved from God's wrath (v. 5:9)
- Reconciled to him (v. 5:10)
- Gift of righteousness (v. 5:17)
- Life (v. 5:18)
- Eternal life (v. 5:21)

You didn't earn any of these things; they are described as gifts and provisions of grace (v. 5:17). How does God feel about you and what does he think about you to give these good things to you?

In this passage the apostle Paul once again compared what you *were* with what you *are* as a follower of Jesus. Look at and meditate on these lists:

WHAT YOU WERE	WHAT YOU ARE
Powerless and ungodly (v. 6)	Valued and loved (vv. 6, 9)
Sinner (v. 8)	Saved (vv. 9, 10)
God's enemy (v. 10)	Reconciled (vv. 10, 11)
Related to Adam (v. 14)	Related to Christ (v. 15)
Judged and condemned (v. 16)	Righteous (vv. 17, 19, 21)

Circle the word in the right-hand column that you most need to accept as your identity today. Choose today to see yourself as God sees you. Fill in the blank:

BY GOD'S GRACE, I AM:

Close in prayer, by coming to God with this identity. Thank God for seeing you as he does, and ask him to help you continue to see yourself this way.

Read John 8:2-11.

THEME VERSE

" … Neither do I condemn you," Jesus declared. "Go now and leave your life of sin" (John 8:11).

How did the teachers of the law and the Pharisees view this woman? What names might they have given to her?

_____

_____

_____

_____

_____

How did Jesus view her? What name would he have called her by?

_____

_____

_____

_____

_____

_____

Put yourself in the story. Imagine you were the one brought in front of the crowd and Jesus after being caught in sin. What would you be feeling as they drag you in front of everyone? As they accuse you? As Jesus speaks to you?

_____

_____

_____

_____

_____

_____

Most churchgoers are very familiar with John 3:16: "For God so loved the world that he gave his one and only Son, that whoever believes in him shall not perish but have eternal life." It's a wonderful verse that we've memorized, heard sermons on, and hold onto as a source of hope.

Not as many people are as familiar with John 3:17-18:

> "For God did not send his Son into the world to condemn the world, but to save the world through him. Whoever believes in him is not condemned, but whoever does not believe stands condemned already because they have not believed in the name of God's one and only Son."

Satan wants to accuse you and condemn you. The world wants to do the same. You may have even experienced other churchgoers condemning you. Yet they have no condemning power over you. God is the only one who can condemn, and when you believe in and belong to Jesus, he looks you in the eye and says, "Neither do I condemn you."

What would happen if everyone understood this truth—that Jesus came to save us, not to condemn us?

_____

_____

_____

_____

_____

Note that Jesus did not give this woman a free pass to continue in her life of sin. He didn't condemn her, but he wanted to save her from her bad decisions. He wanted her to change, to repent, to be transformed. Does he want the same for you today? If so, how?

_____

_____

_____

_____

_____

For your prayer time today, read and meditate on Psalm 51:1-2. Make it your own prayer:

"Have mercy on me, O God,
according to your unfailing love;
according to your great compassion
blot out my transgressions.
Wash away all my iniquity
and cleanse me from my sin."

WEEK FOUR, DAY SIX

Read Colossians 3:1-10.

THEME VERSE
"For you died, and your life is now hidden with Christ in God"
(Colossians 3:3).

The apostle Paul made it clear that when you follow Christ, you are
to put to death all the things that belong to your earthly nature. As
Christ changes you from the inside out, you get rid of all the stuff
that was part of your old way of life. You do this because "you have
taken off your old self with its practices and put on the new self"
(vv. 9-10).

Think of ways you can put to death or rid yourself of the practices
that were part of your old self. What help do you need?

In many cities, churches have started ministries to reach out to
broken women in the community who are involved in the adult
entertainment industry. They seek to introduce the ladies to the gospel and the love of Jesus Christ, praying that the women will allow
Christ to change their lives.

Dave wrote about an experience he and his wife had one Christmas. He said:

> My wife and I partnered with a ministry in our town, and we decided to have a Christmas dinner and party for these girls, who many times have been so wounded by others and overlooked by churches. So the day arrived, and into our home streamed girls, most of whom had found Christ and had hung up their dancing shoes.
>
> There also were a few women who were contemplating attending the ministry's Bible studies and leaving that old life behind. Some were quite uneasy at first, but as time went on, they began to feel safe and loved. When it came time for the meal, they sat down at decorated tables with place settings. Some were nervous, because they had never been to a Christmas dinner. But the longer they were there, the more comfortable they became. Throughout the meal the sound of laughter filled the house, as conversations flowed and relationships were formed and deepened. Gifts provided by a ladies' Bible study were given to each woman, and each was handed a red rose.
>
> One woman had brought a friend who also was a former dancer. I learned that when this woman found out the party was to be at a preacher's house, she became very nervous. She explained that her experience with Christians dated back a couple of decades. When she had entered the club to go to work, a line of Christians stood outside with signs and posters. They had called her names, she said. They had called her a whore and shouted that she was heading to hell.
>
> Her friend in the car said, "Oh, you don't need to worry about that happening. This will be very different."

Before they left the party, a fifteen-minute teaching about the true meaning of Christmas was shared, along with a time of prayer. Those ladies don't pray the way most church people pray. There was no pretense. They had experienced major transformations and left behind a sordid past, and they were pouring their hearts out in prayer. Then I closed the prayer. And in the middle of it I paused, because I wanted to acknowledge how blessed I am to have such a rare wife. So I just said, "And, Lord, I also want to thank you for a wife who allows me to invite dozens of women over to our home for dinner."

The group of girls responded with some "amens," and then one of the young women yelled out, "Stripper girls at that!" Everyone laughed, and I continued with my prayer. But the second I said my final amen, one of the women who is a committed Christian, blurted out, "We're not stripper girls—not anymore. The Bible says we are new creations, daughters of the King!" The Christian women agreed with her. And so did I.

Evidently, that Christian woman wanted to make sure those ladies knew that that is what they *were*, but it was no longer who they *are*.

So, by what name does Satan call you? It might not be "stripper girl." Maybe it's "disengaged wife." Maybe it's "workaholic father." Maybe it's "dishonest employee." Maybe it's "rebellious teenager."

I don't know what title Satan haunts you with, but God offers a pardon for your past, and he calls you a new creation. What happened at that preacher's home around a dinner table is a microcosm of what is happening at Christ's table for each of us on a much larger and eternal scale. The truth is that none of us feel like we deserve a seat at God's table. Why in the world would we be invited? And yet we need to be reminded that he invites us, he welcomes us and he longs for us to trust in him.

Take a moment and print a word or phrase on the nametag that describes who you were. In fact, write as many as you wish!

WHO I WAS

Now, cross out the name(s) on that tag with a large, bold x. If you belong to Christ, those names no longer apply to you.

Next, prayerfully write the name or names that you imagine God calling you by today. Look back through previous days of this week's journals if you need to.

WHO I AM

Praise God your Creator, Savior, Lord and Redeemer. He is the one who made it possible for you to be called by your new name!

WHERE DO I GO WITH MY DISAPPOINTMENT?

HUDDLE UP

PAIN BRINGS PERSEVERANCE

FILM STUDY

STUDY THE PLAYBOOK

John 16:16-33

① What overall perspectives was Jesus conveying to his disciples about suffering? *eventually it will turn to rejoice*

② What kinds of distresses does Jesus say we will experience in the world?

③ Why do you think Jesus chose to reassure the disciples about their relationship with the Father and prayer (vv. 23-28) at this time?

④ What did the disciples' failures reveal about their faith?

⑤ What did they learn, and how did God use their failures to develop and deepen their faith?

⑥ How has God used your troubles and your failures in the past to deepen your faith?

⑦ What is your biggest takeaway from this passage about the purpose of pain in your life?

BREAK THE HUDDLE

How do you explain Jesus' promise of "peace"?

> "Do not be anxious about anything, but in every situation, by prayer and petition, with thanksgiving, present your requests to God. And the peace of God, which transcends all understanding, will guard your hearts and your minds in Christ Jesus" (Philippians 4:6-7).

MEMORY VERSE
"In this world you will have trouble. But take heart! I have overcome the world," (John 16:33).

NEXT
UP

Complete the six sections in the Personal Journal before the next group experience. Use these in your daily time with God over the next six days to help you reflect, evaluate, dig deeper into God's Word and put into practice what you're learning.

WEEK FIVE, DAY ONE

Read Psalm 13.

THEME VERSE
"How long, LORD? Will you forget me forever? How long will you hide your face from me?" (Psalm 13:1)

As Dave mentioned in the video this week, sometimes when we pray, asking God for answers, relief, healing or just some sort of intervention, all we hear is silence.

As you pray to God, you may feel as if he is far away; maybe even that he has deserted you. If you're not careful, you can believe God is not listening to you—maybe to everyone else, but not to you. You might fall into the trap of thinking God does not love you, or that you've done something wrong that has made God turn his back on you.

Does this describe how you feel or have felt? If so, honestly describe what this "silence" has felt like to you.

You are not alone. You are not the only one who has prayed to God and waited for him to answer. On various occasions, David said:

> "Listen to my words, LORD, consider my lament. Hear my cry for help, my King and my God, for to you I pray" (Psalm 5:1-2).

> "Why, LORD, do you stand far off? Why do you hide yourself in times of trouble?" (Psalm 10:1).

> "My God, my God, why have you forsaken me? Why are you so far from saving me, so far from my cries of anguish? My God, I cry out by day, but you do not answer, by night, but I find no rest" (Psalm 22:1-2).

It seems David, the man after God's own heart (1 Samuel 13:14), battled constantly with God's silence. Yet David also wrote some of the most tender and genuine words that have ever been written about his closeness with God (i.e., Psalm 23, 62, 63). David had an honest, humble relationship with God. Even when he was in the desert (physically, emotionally and spiritually), he kept trusting God as his King and Lord.

Look back as Psalm 13. In what ways do you relate to David?

One of the great words in many of David's psalms is the word *but* (v. 5). After David had candidly poured out his heart to God, he gathered himself and looked at the bigger picture. He took his eyes off his circumstances and looked instead to God. In this way, David revealed who he was and whose he was.

What does it take for you to trust in God's unfailing love in the midst of trouble, disappointment and God's silence?

Read through Psalm 13 one more time, this time making it your own prayer. Put David's prayer to God into your own words, honestly pouring your heart out to God and trusting in his unfailing love and goodness.

WEEK FIVE, DAY TWO

Read Hebrews 12:1-12.

THEME VERSE

"Endure hardship as discipline; God is treating you as his children"
(Hebrews 12:7).

In this passage, the writer of Hebrews is giving us a perspective
on suffering that perhaps we don't usually consider. Maybe God
is using this somehow for your good and for his good. Perhaps
there's more to your disappointments, hurts and loss than meets
the eye.

Dave talked about the loss that pitcher Dave Dravecky dealt with
when he was diagnosed with cancer and had his pitching arm
amputated. During this time, God taught Dravecky that the valleys
of life are where all the lush vegetation is; that's where God helps
us grow and deepen in our relationship with him.

Take a few moments to focus on a specific area of disappointment,
suffering or loss in your life. Then consider how God is teaching,
changing or equipping you through this. Write out your thoughts.

Discipline never seems pleasant at the time, but painful. Yet God is treating you as his own child, whom he loves. Joni Eareckson Tada said from the vantage point of her wheelchair, "Sometimes God allows what he hates to accomplish what he loves."

Knowing that God has your best in mind through his discipline, how can you respond differently to hardships? Be as specific as you can! (For more help on this question, read Psalm 6; Proverbs 3:11-12; and Revelation 3:19.)

In a number of his psalms, including Psalm 6, David wrote, "How long, Lord, how long?" How long will this agony and anguish last? How long will you discipline me? How long before you deliver me?

Many Christians have asked those questions, and it's OK to ask them. But you can also recognize that God is working on his own timetable, not yours. He's working for your good, and even as you go through the dark valley, remember that he lovingly walks with you as your Father.

How long? One response is, until you learn what God needs you to learn to become who he wants you to become! "Later on," says Hebrews 12:11, God's discipline will produce "a harvest of righteousness and peace for those who have been trained by it."

A friend who is dealing with a long series of difficulties and disappointments asks you, "How long must I go through this? Where is God?" How would you respond?

In verses 1-4 of Hebrews 12, the writer used Jesus as our model for how to respond to opposition and struggles. Take a few moments to reflect on Jesus as he suffered on the cross. He said, "My God, my God, why have you forsaken me?" (Mark 15:34). Jesus, God's only Son, who was one with the Father in ways we can't even comprehend, felt as if God had deserted him. Try to imagine how Jesus must have felt. As the Father looked down on him on the cross and saw all of our sins that Jesus was taking on himself, God turned away, at least momentarily. Jesus experienced this separation from his Father so that we never have to. "Consider him," says the Hebrews writer, "so that you will not grow weary or lose heart" (Hebrews 12:3).

Close your study time today in prayer, fixing your eyes on Jesus. Again, a secret to dealing with suffering is to take your eyes off your circumstances and to focus on Jesus. During this time, submit to your loving Father, and to his discipline, and live (v. 9)!

WEEK FIVE, DAY THREE

Read John 3:22-36.

THEME VERSE
"He must become greater; I must become less" (John 3:30).

John the Baptist knew who he was and what his calling was. He didn't try to be more than he was; he knew and respected his unique position in God's kingdom. He played his role and left everything else up to God. Over the next two weeks you will study John to see what you can learn from his life.

Describe John the Baptist's attitude toward his life and circumstances.

The people around John began comparing him to Jesus, as if there was a competition taking place. They had a figurative white board on the wall that tracked John's baptisms versus Jesus', and John was falling behind! But for John there was no rivalry; he viewed it as part of God's plan and he saw his ministry through the eyes of stewardship (v. 27). The crowds didn't belong to him in the first place. His power, prestige and self-image didn't depend on the world's view of success.

How do you deal with competition? How does this affect how you deal with disappointments and other struggles in life?

How has the way you've viewed "your" life and "your" success influenced how you deal with disappointments in life?

You may or may not have been given stewardship over crowds of people as John was, but God has given you stewardship over other things. What can you learn from John about how to view the following as gifts given from heaven rather than sources of your success?

"YOUR" CAREER

"YOUR" FINANCES

"YOUR" CHILDREN

"YOUR" HEALTH

"YOUR" GIFTS AND ABILITIES

What does it mean to you for Jesus to become greater and greater and for you to become less and less?

Through John's reply (vv. 27-36), he pointed to Jesus as the one who is preeminent (superior, all-surpassing). The Father "has placed everything in his hands" (v. 35). As you close in prayer, worship Jesus as the all-surpassing Bridegroom (his church is his bride). As you pray, mindfully place him above all. Ask him for his power to be his witness so he may become greater as you become less.

WEEK FIVE, DAY FOUR

Read Luke 7:18-35.

THEME VERSE

When the men came to Jesus, they said, "John the Baptist sent us to you to ask, 'Are you the one who is to come, or should we expect someone else?'" (Luke 7:20)

In the movie presentation this past week, we saw several people go through a season of uncertainty. Loss, criticism, hostilities, wounds, disappointment—they can all lead to times of discouragement and doubt.

Yesterday you studied John the Baptist and saw his faith even when his ministry began to decline. At that time, John was still certain about his identity and the identity of Jesus. He had earlier identified Jesus as "the Lamb of God, who takes away the sin of the world" (John 1:29; see also v. 36). He said, "I have seen and I testify that this is God's Chosen One" (v. 34). You can't get any clearer than that!

It seems that John would be the last person on earth to be uncertain about the identity of Jesus Christ. But just as in our own lives, sometimes when circumstances change, uncertainty gradually begins to replace certainty. The devil's darts of doubt disillusion our discerning of the divine. John kept preaching—now to a smaller audience. One day he was preaching, he called out the king for an immoral relationship and told him to repent. The king responded by throwing John into prison. As Jesus' popularity was increasing, John was rotting in a jail cell. That's when he asked his followers to go and make sure Jesus really was the One. And, by the way, it appears John was also questioning his own identity, because if Jesus wasn't who John thought he was, all of John's ministry would have been in vain.

You may not be sitting in a jail cell. Your circumstances are probably much different, but you can still feel those darts of doubt creeping in—or sitting with all their weight on your chest. What do those darts of doubt look like to you?

Honest doubt can be an act of integrity. God loves honest seekers. There are times when many of us, if not all of us, struggle with doubts. Author and Pastor Stephen Brown said, "If you've never had a question about your faith, you probably don't have much faith." Evangelist and teacher Oswald Chambers said, "Doubt is not always a sign that a man is wrong; it may be a sign that he is thinking." Philosopher Francis Bacon said, "If we begin with certainties, we will end in doubt. But if we begin with doubts, and bear them patiently, we may end in certainty."

Jude 1:22 says, "Be merciful to those who doubt." Why? Because if you're patient with honest doubters, in time they will become strong believers.

What role has doubt played (or is it playing) in the growth of your faith?

_____

_____

_____

_____

_____

Being a Christian means that at times you will have doubts to work through. A faith that has never been tested cannot be trusted. An oak tree doesn't grow strong if it never encounters wind, storms and elements. It is adversity that allows it to grow, thrive, strengthen and flourish.

Notice that John the Baptist didn't just sit and sulk, and he didn't just have some philosophical debate with the disciples. He sent word to Jesus and had his friends ask, "Are you the one who was to come, or should we expect someone else?"

Doubt should drive you to go on a spiritual search for truth. Dig into God's Word with your questions. Put it to the test. If you are going through a period of doubt right now, ask your tough questions in your small group, with an individual from your group, a teacher or a minister.

How will you follow up on any doubts you have? What are your next steps?

_____

_____

_____

_____

_____

_____

You can start right now as you pray. Take your uncertainties to God right now. Just be honest with him. Ask him to help you in your doubts. If you are not struggling with any doubts right now, spend your prayer time interceding for someone you know who is.

_____

_____

_____

_____

WEEK FIVE, DAY FIVE

Read Romans 12:9-21.

THEME VERSE

"Be devoted to one another in love. Honor one another above yourselves" (Romans 12:10).

How do you deal with disappointments and setbacks and loss? As Dave mentioned in the video, it's a good thing you're involved in a circle of Christian friends who can lift you up. And it's good for them that you're in the group—so you can lift *them* up! Your group is a tremendous asset for each person in it as you walk through the ups and downs of life together. That's exactly what God intended as he built the church. As Paul said in Romans 12:5, "each member belongs to all the others."

Consider what that statement implies: you belong to one another. How well is your church and group living out that value?

In Romans 12:9-21, Paul spelled out what belonging to each other looks like. Honestly evaluate yourself, your church or your small group on each of these instructions for community life.

-2 = we do just the opposite of this
0 = we really don't do this at all
2 = we excel at this.

"Be devoted to one another in love" (Romans 12:10a).

-2   -1   0   1   2

"Honor one another above yourselves" (Romans 12:10b).

-2   -1   0   1   2

"Never be lacking in zeal, but keep your spiritual fervor, serving the Lord," (Romans 11).

-2   -1   0   1   2

"Be joyful in hope" (Romans 12a).

-2   -1   0   1   2

"Be patient in affliction" (Romans 12b).

-2   -1   0   1   2

"Be faithful in prayer" (Romans 12c).

-2   -1   0   1   2

"Share with the Lord's people who are in need" (Romans 12:13a).

-2   -1   0   1   2

"Practice hospitality" (Romans 12:13b).

-2	-1	0	1	2

"Bless those who persecute you; bless and do not curse" (Romans 12:14).

-2	-1	0	1	2

"Rejoice with those who rejoice; mourn with those who mourn" (Romans 12:15).

-2	-1	0	1	2

"Live in harmony with one another" (Romans 12:16a).

-2	-1	0	1	2

"Do not be proud, but be willing to associate with people of low position. Do not be conceited" (Romans 12:16b).

-2	-1	0	1	2

"Do not repay anyone evil for evil" (Romans 12:17a).

-2	-1	0	1	2

"Be careful to do what is right in the eyes of everyone" (Romans 12:17b).

-2	-1	0	1	2

"If it is possible, as far as it depends on you, live at peace with everyone" (Romans 12:18).

-2	-1	0	1	2

"Do not take revenge, my dear friends, but leave room for God's wrath" (Romans 12:19).

| -2 | -1 | 0 | 1 | 2 |

"Do not be overcome by evil, but overcome evil with good" (Romans 12:21).

| -2 | -1 | 0 | 1 | 2 |

Look at all your responses. Overall, how are you, your group and your church doing at living in biblical community?

_____

_____

_____

_____

_____

_____

In other places in the New Testament, we find instructions such as these:

" ... Spur one another on toward love and good deeds" (Hebrews 10:24).

" ... Teach and admonish one another with all wisdom ... " (Colossians 3:16).

"Carry each other's burdens ... " (Galatians 6:2).

" … Confess your sins to each other and pray for each other so that you may be healed" (James 5:16).

" … Speak the truth in love, growing in every way more and more like Christ … " (Ephesians 4:15, NLT).

As Dave said, we need people to speak truth into our lives. Sometimes we don't need a pat on the back as much as we need a kick in the pants! Your small group should be a safe place, a loving place for that to happen.

What "tough love" do you need from your group right now?

_____

_____

_____

What is your responsibility in speaking the truth in love in your group?

_____

_____

_____

_____

"Pray for each other so that you may be healed." Pray for your group members today. Pray for their needs, especially as related to dealing with disappointments, struggles and suffering. Afterward, phone a group member or two and offer to pray for them.

Read James 1:2-8, 12-18.

THEME VERSE

"Consider it pure joy, my brothers and sisters, whenever you face trials of many kinds ... " (James 1:2).

James couldn't really have meant what he said, could he? Consider it a joy when you face trials?

What is your first reaction to equating trials with joy?

The trials themselves may not be very joyful, but what they will produce in you will. These trials will test your faith, he says, which will develop perseverance in you. That means you can hold up under these trials over the long haul! This doesn't seem to be getting any better. But perseverance will do its job—as you hold onto your faith over years of struggle and disappointment—so you will become mature in your faith. Aha! That's what God is doing in you.

Perhaps James and the apostle Paul discussed this principle at some time in the past (Galatians 1:19; 2:9) or maybe the Holy Spirit inspired them similarly. James talked about becoming "mature and complete, not lacking anything." Paul talked about becoming " … mature, attaining to the whole measure of the fullness of Christ" (Ephesians 4:13). They're both saying the same thing. Your maturity is God's end game, and he'll do whatever it takes for as long as it takes to get you there.

The question is, will you allow God to do whatever it takes? As discussed in Lesson 4, God's part is transformation; your job is surrender. Both God's part and your part are necessary to bring maturity. Will you allow God to do whatever it takes for as long as it takes? Write out your surrender agreement below. (By the way, this surrender is completely on God's terms and it is unconditional on your part!)

Spiritual maturity means you become more and more like Christ (Ephesians 4:13, 15; Romans 8:29; 2 Peter 3:18). In what ways do you want to become more like Christ?

_____

_____

_____

Stephen Brown said, "For every unbeliever who gets cancer, God allows a believer to get cancer so the world can see the difference."

How would you apply that idea to an area of disappointment or suffering in your life? How can God be glorified by the difference in how you handle it?

_____

_____

_____

_____

_____

_____

Here's some more good news. When you surrender to God and he does his transforming work in you, James says you will " … receive the crown of life that the Lord has promised to those who love him (James 1:12). While your maturity is his more immediate goal for you, his larger goal is victory; the victor gets the crown of life. Victor over what? Over all the trials of this life! Your trials and your crown are good and perfect gifts from the Father (James 1:17).

That's a reason to celebrate! That's a reason for pure joy!

Close this session's personal studies in prayer, thanking God for the way he's working in you to develop you into the person he wants you to become.

WHAT WILL MY LEGACY BE?

GROUP TIME

HUDDLE UP

How have you seen God do what was unlikely, or even "impossible" by human standards, to carry out his will?

FILM STUDY

STUDY THE PLAYBOOK

1 Timothy 1:12-19

1. Why might Paul be considered an unlikely person to be used by God to preach the gospel and bring revival?

2. How was Paul an example for others to follow?

3. What do you think prompted Paul to break out into spontaneous worship (v. 17)?

4. If you were Timothy, how would you receive Paul's words of blessing?

   "You then, my son, be strong in the grace that is in Christ Jesus. And the things you have heard me say in the presence of many witnesses entrust to reliable people who will also be qualified to teach others" (2 Timothy 2:1-2).

5. Who comes to mind when you think about the legacy of faith you will leave?

BREAK THE HUDDLE

Will God bring revival today? How will you live so it begins with you?

MEMORY VERSE
"Now to the King eternal, immortal, invisible, the only God, be honor and glory for ever and ever. Amen" (1 Timothy 1:17).

NEXT
UP

Complete the six sections in the *Personal Journal*. Use them in your daily time with God over the next week to help you reflect, evaluate, dig deeper into God's Word and put into practice what you're learning.

WEEK SIX, DAY ONE

Read Habakkuk 3.

THEME VERSE

"Lord, I have heard of your fame; I stand in awe of your deeds, Lord. Repeat them in our day, in our time make them known" (Habakkuk 3:2).

In the previous chapters of this Bible book we see the prophet Habakkuk move from worry (1:2-4) to watching (2:1) and waiting (2:3) to worship (2:20; 3:1-2, 18) and finally to witness (3:19). His witness flowed out of his heart for God, no matter how bad the circumstances were. That's the same process many Christians go through as they faithfully face fear and adversity.

Think back through how you've faced a disappointment, struggle or loss and the process you went through. How did you work through each of these stages? (Or perhaps you are in the middle of this process. If so, where are you now, and where do you think you need to go from here?)

WORRY → WATCHING → WAITING → WORSHIP → WITNESS

_____

_____

_____

_____

_____

_____

Habakkuk looked around him and saw the impending invasion of a ruthless enemy. He looked inside himself and felt the pounding of his heart and quivering lips. He felt so weak it was as if his bones were decaying. He could feel his legs trembling beneath him. He was frightened to his very core at what was about to occur. Yet he looked up and trusted his God no matter what happened.

Complete the following phrases to describe yourself:

RIGHT NOW, AS I LOOK AROUND AT THE WORLD AND MY CIRCUMSTANCES, I SEE ...

WHEN I LOOK INSIDE MYSELF, I FEEL ...

WHEN I LOOK UP TO GOD, I KNOW ...

What does it look like for you to "wait patiently" for God in the midst of your circumstances?

_____

_____

_____

_____

The theme verse for today is an incredible prayer of worship over the things God has done in the past and a request for him to do it again in our time. Each day this week you will pray this prayer for a modern-day revival. Begin today to pray this powerful prayer:

> LORD, I have heard of your fame;
> I stand in awe of your deeds, LORD.
> Repeat them in our day,
>   in our time make them known;
>   in wrath remember mercy.

WEEK SIX, DAY TWO

Read Psalm 145.

THEME VERSE
"One generation commends your works to another; they tell of your mighty acts" (Psalm 145:4).

The Bible is replete with instructions to tell the next generation about God and his mighty works from the past. (To study this further, see Psalm 48:13; 71:18; 78:1-8; 79:13; 102:18; Exodus 3:15; 12:1-42.) It's vital for us to hand down our faith to the next generation, whether that's our children, grandchildren, nieces, nephews or anyone else God places in our spheres of influence. Write a list, below, of who is in the "next generation" for you.

_____

_____

_____

_____

_____

_____

_____

That could be a rather large list! As you look at those names, who does God most put on your heart to pray for and tell of God's mighty works? List one to three names.

That is, when they would start God's might to be confident, this

Take a moment now and pray for these individuals by name. Ask the Father to draw them to him. Ask Jesus to make himself real to them. Ask the Holy Spirit to convict them of their need for God.

Read through this psalm again and write down every word that describes who God is.

_____

_____

_____

_____

_____

_____

Take a moment and, as verse 5 says, meditate on who God is and what he does.

Look at your list above of attributes for God. Circle the ones that most stand out to you.

This psalm is not only a song of worship—it's also a testimony to others about God's greatness and love, his power and mercy. We can't help but tell others about this God. As you go through your day today, how will you tell others (through your words and actions) about who God is?

_____

_____

_____

_____

_____

_____

_____

_____

_____

_____

_____

Close your time in prayer. Use Psalm 145's descriptions of God and what he has done in the past as reasons to worship him.

> Lord, I've heard of your fame. I stand in awe of you and your deeds …

> Lord, do it again! Bring revival to our city … nation … world. Do what you did in Birmingham in the 70s and in Jerusalem, Judea and surrounding areas in the first century. Lord, repeat your mighty deeds in our day. Make them known in our time!

WEEK SIX, DAY THREE

Read Genesis 48:8-21.

THEME VERSE
"Now Israel's eyes were failing because of old age, and he could hardly see. So Joseph brought his sons close to him, and his father kissed them and embraced them" (Genesis 48:10).

One of the most memorable scenes from last week's video presentation was when Tony Nathan's father spoke to him in the locker room just before the start of the rivalry game with Banks. "Look at me," he said to his son. "I'm proud of you." This was a powerful example of the biblical principle of giving a blessing to your child. Everyone needs to hear this kind of blessing from a parent, coach, teacher, pastor or fellow group member.

Reflect on a time when a parent or someone else in your life gave you a blessing like this. What did they say? What were the circumstances? How did it make you feel?

_____

_____

_____

_____

_____

_____

_____

Jacob, also known as Israel, blessed his son, Joseph (49:22-26), as well as Joseph's two children. Don't get caught up in whom he blessed first—that's a lesson for another time—but look at the tenderness and truth of Jacob's words. Why is it significant to give a blessing to your children or grandchildren, or receive one from your parents or grandparents?

_____

_____

_____

_____

_____

Who needs to hear words of blessing from you today? What will you say?

_____

_____

I grew up in a preacher's home. My father was busy with a demanding schedule, but he always made time for family. One day my dad received a telephone call from the preacher of a large, well-known church. As I listened from the other room, it was obvious Dad was being asked to come and speak. His excitement was evident. "February 3? I'd love to. First let me check my calendar."

He went bounding up the stairs to get his calendar, and as he did, my heart sank. February 3 was the night of a program at my middle school, and I had a significant part in it.

Dad returned to the kitchen wall phone, flipping through the pages of his appointment booklet. At last I heard him say, "February 3? No, I'm sorry, but I already have a commitment on that evening. Maybe some other time."

Without saying a single word to me, he communicated his availability, love and support. I was his commitment, and nothing could entice him away from an appointment with his son.

Words are vital for giving a blessing to people you love, but sometimes your actions bless even louder than words. What do your actions say about your love and commitment to the people you love? How do your actions either bless or curse the people you love?

Close in prayer, asking God to use you to bless others. Pray specifically by name for those you love: your children, grandchildren, parents, grandparents, spouse or others. Pray God's blessing on them today. Then pray for God to bring revival in your family and others you love. Ask him to make himself and his deeds known to them. "Repeat them in our day, Lord!"

WEEK SIX, DAY FOUR

Read Ephesians 5:8-20.

THEME VERSE

"Be very careful, then, how you live—not as unwise but as wise, making the most of every opportunity" (Ephesians 5:15-16).

Darkness and light—this contrast is a major theme throughout the Bible. The first mention of it is in the first four verses of the first book of the Bible:

> "In the beginning God created the heavens and the earth. Now the earth was formless and empty, darkness was over the surface of the deep, and the Spirit of God was hovering over the waters. And God said, 'Let there be light,' and there was light. God saw that the light was good, and he separated the light from the darkness" (Genesis 1:1-4).

The last mention is in the last chapter of the Bible, as the new heaven and new earth are described:

> "There will be no more night. They will not need the light of a lamp or the light of the sun, for the Lord God will give them light. And they will reign for ever and ever" (Revelation 22:5).

Jesus was described as the "light of the world" (John 8:12). In fact, the apostle John introduced him as light, as opposed to darkness, in his gospel:

"In him was life, and that life was the light of all mankind. The light shines in the darkness, and the darkness has not overcome it" (John 1:4-5).

That Jesus is the "light of the world" may be no big surprise to you. But during the Sermon on the Mount, Jesus looked at his followers and said,

> "*You* are the light of the world. A town built on a hill cannot be hidden. Neither do people light a lamp and put it under a bowl. Instead they put it on its stand, and it gives light to everyone in the house. In the same way, let your light shine before others, that they may see your good deeds and glorify your Father in heaven" (Matthew 5:14-16, emphasis added).

That's what the apostle Paul meant in the passage under consideration today: " … You were once in darkness … " That is what you *were*. But "*now* you are light in the Lord." So, he says, you are to live in the light and have nothing to do with the fruitless, shameful deeds of darkness.

In what ways do you see yourself as the light of the Lord in the world?

Think about the scene in the video in which Hank spoke at the rally and the crowd lit candles to symbolize the fact that the life of each Christ follower is significant in bringing light to a dark world. In what areas of "darkness" in your world is God placing you as a light?

_____

_____

_____

_____

_____

_____

Banks quarterback Jeff Rutledge told Tony Nathan, "Go where you can make the most difference." That's a vital part of how God uses us to bring about revival today. God can use you to make a difference in the world, right where you are now or perhaps somewhere else. How? "Be very careful, then, how you live—not as unwise but as wise, making the most of every opportunity … " (Ephesians 5:15-16).

What opportunity do you have in the next few days that you can make the most of?

_____

_____

_____

_____

God can light a fire in you, and he can use you as a light in a dark place to bring revival today. Pray that he will help you wisely make the most of every opportunity he gives you to bring revival. Ask him for the opportunity today to tell others of his fame and his awesome deeds. Ask him to use an ordinary person like you to repeat past revivals in your day.

WEEK SIX, DAY FIVE

Read John 14:1-14.

THEME VERSES

"I am the way and the truth and the life. No one comes to the Father except through me" (John 14:6).

" ... whoever believes in me will do the works I have been doing, and they will do even greater things than these, because I am going to the Father" (John 14:12).

Imagine for a moment that you were one of Jesus' disciples, and he—your rabbi and friend, who you've been following for three years—has just told you that he is leaving (John 13:33). You had given up everything, including your career, to be in this group. Now he says he's going, and where he's going you cannot go.

If you were one of these men, what would you have been thinking and feeling?

_____

_____

_____

_____

The original purpose of Jesus' words in today's study was to explain to his disciples where he was going, what he'd be doing, and how they could carry on once he was physically gone. We're still in the same circumstances they were after he left. His words of comfort and clarification to them are for us, as well.

Part of Jesus' clarification is contained in John 14:6, a verse you have probably heard many times before, if you've been around the church for very long. It's been a theme verse for this entire series. Jesus was saying, in effect, that there is ONE WAY to the Father, and he is that one way. He is also the truth; that is, the true revelation of the Father. In him there is absolutely no falseness. And he is the life—life to the full in the here and now and life eternally through our faith in him. Skeptics see Jesus' statement (and ours, when we repeat it) as intolerant of other "ways," but Jesus was simply clarifying God's plan.

How does Jesus' clarification that he is the only way to the Father (rather than by doing good works or through various religions or beliefs) bring comfort?

_____

_____

_____

_____

When Jesus said "I am the way, the truth, and the life," he was declaring that he was the great "I AM," that is, God Almighty. He is "far above all rule and authority, power and dominion, and every name that is invoked, not only in the present age but also in the one to come" (Ephesians 1:21). While on Earth, he changed water into wine, calmed storms, walked on water, healed the sick and loved the unlovable. Yet he said, "Whoever believes in me will do the works I have been doing, and they will do even greater things than these, because I am going to the Father" (John 14:12).

Now, before you go out and try to walk across the top of the water in your swimming pool, know that these greater works involve things like reaching lost people with the gospel. On the Day of Pentecost, Peter preached a sermon and 3,000 people responded and were baptized. That was a great work—something even Jesus had never done during his earthly ministry years! Sharing the Good News with your nonbelieving friends and seeing them give their life to Jesus as the way, the truth and the life is also a great work. There is perhaps no greater work than to see God move powerfully through an ordinary believer to transform the life of an unbeliever. And don't forget that "it is *God* who works in you to will and to act in order to fulfill his good purpose" (Philippians 2:13, emphasis added).

When Jesus responds to your prayers as you carry out the work he has given you, he says the Father is glorified in the Son (John 14:13). It's another way of pointing up to the only One who can save. It's another way of saying, "Not to us, Lord, not to us but to your name be the glory, because of your love and faithfulness" (Psalm 115:1). As you live as a witness and do your work, how will you make sure God receives the glory instead of you?

_____

_____

_____

_____

_____

Because Jesus has gone to the Father, you can ask him anything in his name. He is the ever-present God who is all-powerful. With that in mind, what do you want to pray for today? Remember, you can ask for *anything*, as long as it is …

- something Jesus would ask for
- something that matches up with his purposes
- something that would please him and bring glory to the Father

He " … is able to do immeasurably more than all we ask or imagine, according to his power that is at work within us … " (Ephesians 3:20). So what will you imagine? For what will you ask? (Use the three qualifiers above.)

_____

_____

_____

_____

_____

_____

_____

One of the things we know for certain that God wants is revival—for people to return to him and give their lives to him. Pray for God to IGNITE that revival now.

> "God, I've heard what our ancestors say about you, and I'm stopped in my tracks, down on my knees. Do among us what you did among them. Work among us as you worked among them. And as you bring judgment, as you surely must, remember mercy (Habakkuk 3:2, *The Message*).

WEEK SIX, DAY SIX

Read 2 Timothy 4:1-8.

THEME VERSE
"Now there is in store for me the crown of righteousness, which the Lord, the righteous Judge, will award to me on that day—and not only to me, but also to all who have longed for his appearing" (2 Timothy 4:8).

On Day One of this week's studies, you looked at part of the first chapter from Paul's letter to his "son in the faith," Timothy. Today, you will investigate the last chapter from his second letter to this young man. Paul was sitting in a jail cell as he wrote this letter to Timothy (1 Corinthians 4:17) He was waiting to be executed. This letter is the last writing we have from Paul.

Someone's last words are usually very significant. When that person is the great missionary Paul, these are words we should pay close attention to!

If you were in Paul's place, waiting in a jail to be executed for your faith in Jesus, who would you write a letter to? What would it say?

_____

_____

_____

_____

_____

_____

_____

_____

_____

_____

_____

_____

_____

Look at verses 2 Timothy: 3-4. How are circumstances like or unlike those in Paul's and Timothy's day?

_____

_____

_____

_____

Look at Paul's instructions to his son in the faith:

PREACH THE WORD (V. 2)

BE PREPARED IN SEASON AND OUT OF SEASON (WHEN IT'S CON-
VENIENT OR NOT, WHEN YOU FEEL LIKE IT OR NOT, WHEN THE TIME
SEEMS RIPE FOR REVIVAL AND WHEN IT DOESN'T)...

CORRECT AND REBUKE

ENCOURAGE

KEEP YOUR HEAD IN ALL SITUATIONS (V. 5)

ENDURE HARDSHIP

DO THE WORK OF AN EVANGELIST

DISCHARGE ALL THE DUTIES OF YOUR MINISTRY

- Which of these come natural to you? Place a 1 next to those.
- Which seem somewhat difficult for you? Place a 2 next to those.
- Which seem impossible under your own power? Place a 3 next
  to those.

Read and reflect on verses 6-8 again. Read it as if you were Paul's
son in the faith, a person he loved dearly.
How did Paul view his impending death?

How would you describe Paul's legacy?

_____

_____

_____

_____

_____

_____

An epitaph is a "commemorative inscription on a tomb or mortuary monument about the person buried at that site" (Dictionary.com).

Throughout these six lessons, you have looked at your life in view of the bigger picture, in view of the revival God desires for his world and your part in it. With that in mind, part of Paul's epitaph might read like this:

> *I have fought the good fight, I have finished the race, I have kept the faith.*

Write out your own epitaph in 15 words or less.

_____

_____

_____

_____

_____

_____

Look again at the list of Paul's instructions to Timothy. Pray for God to empower you in the areas where you marked yourself as a 2 or 3.

Then pray once more for revival.

> "I have heard all about you, LORD. I am filled with awe by your amazing works. In this time of our deep need, help us again as you did in years gone by" (Habakkuk 3:2, NLT).

> "Now to him who is able to do immeasurably more than all we ask or imagine, according to his power that is at work within us, to him be glory in the church and in Christ Jesus throughout all generations, for ever and ever! Amen" (Ephesians 3:20-21).

NOTES